WEIRD WORLD

WEIRD INVENTIONS

BY EMMA KAISER

Core Library

An Imprint of Abdo Publishing
abdobooks.com

Cover Image: The popularity of the bicycle inspired some inventors to create monowheels.

abdobooks.com

Published by Abdo Publishing, a division of ABDO, PO Box 398166, Minneapolis, Minnesota 55439.

Core Library™ is a trademark and logo of Abdo Publishing.

Printed in the United States of America, North Mankato, Minnesota.
102025
012026

Cover Photo: Fox Photos/Hulton Archive/Getty Images
Interior Photos: Claudio Divizia/Shutterstock Images, 4–5; Art Collection/Alamy, 7; Fox Photos/Hulton Archive/Getty Images, 10–11, 30, 43; Shutterstock Images, 13 (top), 13 (bottom), 32–33, 36 (middle left), 36 (middle right), 36 (bottom middle), 36 (bottom right); Kateryna Leonets/Shutterstock Images, 13 (middle); Grzegorz Czapski/Alamy, 14; Underwood Archives/Archive Photos/Getty Images, 17; H. Armstrong Roberts/ClassicStock/Alamy, 18–19; Bettmann/Getty Images, 21; Andrey Popov/Shutterstock Images, 24–25; Fabrice Coffrini/AFP/Getty Images, 27; BNA Photographic/Alamy, 28, 45; Hulton Archive/Archive Photos/Getty Images, 35; Mariia Mazaeva/Shutterstock Images, 36 (top); Victoria Sergeeva/Shutterstock Images, 36 (bottom left); ilbusca/DigitalVision Vectors/Getty Images, 39

Editor: Riley Madsen
Series Designer: Marley Richmond

Library of Congress Control Number: 2025939169

Publisher's Cataloging-in-Publication Data

Names: Kaiser, Emma, author.
Title: Weird inventions / by Emma Kaiser
Description: Minneapolis, Minnesota: Abdo Publishing, 2026 | Series: Weird world | Includes online resources and index.
Identifiers: ISBN 9781098298487 (lib. bdg.) | ISBN 9798384932284 (ebook)
Subjects: LCSH: Oddities--Juvenile literature. | Inventions--Juvenile literature. | Applied science--Juvenile literature. | Technology--Juvenile literature. | Discoveries in science--History--Juvenile literature. | Curiosities and wonders--Juvenile literature.
Classification: DDC 600--dc23

CONTENTS

WALKING ON WATER

In the late 1400s, an Italian man named Leonardo da Vinci puzzled over a sketchbook. He was working on an idea for his latest invention. Leonardo always carried a notebook. He never knew when inspiration might strike.

One day, as Leonardo walked along a lakeshore, he considered whether it was possible to walk on water. He knew about the principle of buoyancy. This principle says that for an object to float, it has to displace a volume of water that weighs at least as much as the object itself.

A statue of Leonardo da Vinci stands outside a museum in Vienna, Austria.

Leonardo wondered if he could create shoes that balanced out a person's weight, allowing the person to walk on water. In his notebook, Leonardo sketched an image of a man wearing water shoes and holding poles in his hands that would help propel him forward.

Leonardo was an artist, scientist, and engineer. His notebook held sketches and ideas for many inventions. Besides his water shoes, Leonardo's ideas for inventions included a submarine, a helicopter, a parachute, and an automobile. Most of his inventions were never actually tested or fully realized. There's no evidence that his water shoes were ever built or used. But his designs were still far ahead of his time.

WATER BICYCLES

In the late 1800s and early 1900s, people became interested in biking on water. Many types of water bicycles were invented. One type had a series of flotation devices so that it could be used on land and in water. Some floated on top of the water with a raft-like base. Some sat partly in the water like a boat with pedals underwater. Many water bikes were patented, but most fell out of popularity.

Leonardo's notebook of ideas became a source of inspiration for many inventors who came after him.

WEIRD INVENTIONS

Inventions are human-made machines or creations that are meant to solve problems or make life easier. Some inventions have changed the course of history. The invention of the printing press made literature more accessible to people than ever before, changing how new ideas were spread. The electric light bulb allowed people to have light at all times of the day. The internet now connects people all around the world.

But not all inventions change history on this scale. Some inventions turn out a bit odd. This may be because they're attempting to solve a problem that isn't really that serious. Or it may be because they try to solve problems in strange or confusing ways. Some inventions seem like good ideas but don't actually work that well. Since the invention of the wheel, people have been creating tools to make life easier. But sometimes they end up making life a little weirder too.

LEONARDO'S ROBOTIC KNIGHT

Few of Leonardo da Vinci's inventions were constructed. But one did make it out of his notebook. Leonardo's robotic metal knight was displayed in the court of Milan, Italy, in 1495. It was operated by pulleys and levers that made the knight's body move. Leonardo had a deep knowledge of the human body and how it worked. He designed the knight to be as much like a human as possible. Leonardo intended for the knight to be a war weapon, but most people just found it entertaining to watch.

STRAIGHT TO THE SOURCE

Leonardo da Vinci included all kinds of thoughts in his notebooks. In one entry, he compared human inventions to nature. He wrote:

> *Though human ingenuity may make various inventions . . . it will never devise any inventions more beautiful, nor more simple, nor more to the purpose than Nature does; because in her inventions nothing is wanting, and nothing is superfluous, and she needs no counterpoise when she makes limbs proper for motion in the bodies of animals.*

Source: Leonardo da Vinci. *The Notebooks of Leonardo da Vinci—Complete*. Translated by Jean Paul Richter, Project Gutenberg, 2004, gutenberg.org. Accessed 20 Aug. 2025.

BACK IT UP

The author of this passage is using evidence to support a point. Write a paragraph describing the point the author is making. Then write down two or three pieces of evidence the author uses to make the point.

CHAPTER TWO

VEHICLES AND TRANSPORTATION

For thousands of years, people have been finding new ways to get around. In 1818, the first bicycle patent was granted, and people quickly began to make every kind of bicycle variation imaginable. Then came more advanced vehicles, such as automobiles and eventually airplanes. Some of these inventions have made travel faster, safer, and more efficient. Other inventions were more flashy than practical.

Because the bicycle became so popular, some inventors tried to create a vehicle with one wheel

Multiple inventors attempted to create their own versions of the monowheel.

PATENTS

A patent grants special rights to an inventor for an invention. It gives an inventor legal protection. This means that others can't make, use, or sell the invention without giving the inventor credit. Patents can also make information about inventions available to the public. This means people can read about and learn from the invention's technology. To patent an invention, inventors have to apply to a government intellectual property office to approve it.

instead of two. It was called a monowheel. A monowheel is different from a unicycle. To drive a unicycle, the rider sits above the wheel. To drive a monowheel, the rider sits inside the wheel. The vehicle looks a bit like a hamster wheel.

The first monowheel was invented in 1869 in France. It was powered by foot pedals. Later versions of the monowheel were powered by engines. The engine was also positioned inside the wheel with the driver. These types of monowheels could reach speeds of 25 to 30 miles per hour (40–48 kmh). However, handling them was difficult.

TYPES OF PATENTS

There are three main types of patents in the United States. Each type protects a different kind of invention. Can you come up with more examples of each type of patent?

Utility Patents

- Protects new products, machines, or processes
- Examples: light bulbs, vacuum cleaners, batteries

Design Patents

- Protects unique designs of a product, such as its shape or pattern
- Examples: a bottle shape or a shoe design

Plant Patents

- Protects new kinds or varieties of certain plants
- Examples: a new variety of apple or carrot

Goodyear's glowing tires were designed to come in a variety of colors, including red, green, orange, and blue.

Because they could tip easily, monowheels were difficult to turn and stop. Some people still own and drive monowheels for fun. But they aren't a very practical way to get around.

GLOWING TIRES

In the early 1960s, the company Goodyear Tires came out with a new product. The company believed it would totally change how people drove their cars. It had invented tires that glowed. First, researchers at the company developed a method for dyeing their tires different colors. Then they attached small light bulbs to the inside of the tire rims. This meant that the tires could glow, especially while driving at night.

THE CAR CATCHER

In the 1930s, streets became crowded with cars. This meant that more and more people were getting hit by cars. An invention called the car catcher or the safety scoop was meant to prevent pedestrians from being hit. The device looked like a giant shovel or scoop attached to the front of the car. It was meant to sweep the pedestrian out of the way. To open the scoop, the driver had to pull a lever. The design never worked well and didn't become popular.

Goodyear hoped people would buy tires to match their cars. The company wanted the colors to match the style of individual drivers. It thought glowing tires would make cars safer by making them easier to see. But after working on the product for ten years, Goodyear's engineers gave up. To dye the tires, they had to melt the rubber at a lower temperature. This made the tires weaker. They broke and tore more easily. They also didn't grip the road as well as ordinary tires, so they didn't perform well in bad weather. While some people witnessed public test drives, the glowing tires never made it to consumers.

THE PRAMOTOR

In 1923, a new kind of vehicle was invented. In the United Kingdom, a baby carriage is called a pram. For parents who didn't want to walk behind a pram, the pramotor made the job a lot easier. The pramotor consisted of a motorized scooter attached to a baby carriage. The person operating the vehicle stood on a platform behind the baby.

The pramotor had a 21-horsepower engine and could be operated at two speeds. However, the vehicle was banned from walking paths in the United Kingdom. This meant it had to be driven on roads. Horse-drawn

One version of the pramotor included a seat for the operator.

carriages, as well as newer automobiles, made roads dangerous places for the pramotor. It soon fell out of style for safety reasons.

COSMETIC INVENTIONS

People have always been interested in improving their image and appearance. Trends in clothing and cosmetics have changed constantly throughout history. Many inventions try to keep up with those trends. They offer products that promise to help people look and feel better. But some inventions made promises that were too good to be true.

Modern gyms are filled with all kinds of machines to help people work out. But one machine from the 1950s guaranteed fat loss

The vibrating belt was supposed to reduce fat from specific areas of the body, but it didn't work because targeted fat reduction is not possible.

without actually having to exercise. Its inventor was John Harvey Kellogg, who helped invent flaked breakfast cereal. Vibrating exercise belts were meant to simply jiggle the fat away. The belts were worn around the waist, legs, arms, or other parts of the body.

The belts may have felt a little like a pleasant massage. They may have even helped with joint pain or poor blood circulation. But vibration has no effect on fat loss. The machines didn't help people lose weight as was advertised. By the 1980s, the machines were no longer in use.

ELECTRIC SHOCK

Some people thought fat could be zapped away. A machine called the Relax-A-Cizor was invented in 1949. It involved belts that were worn around the body. A machine then delivered mild electric shocks through the belts. More than 400,000 Relax-A-Cizors were sold before they were discontinued in 1970. In some cases, the shocks caused or worsened health problems such as abnormal heartbeats and epilepsy.

Evangeline Isabella Gilbert claimed that wearing the dimpler for an hour per day would give the wearer permanent dimples, but it wasn't true.

DIMPLE-MAKING DEVICE

During the 1920s and 1930s, dimples were a popular physical trait. Dimples are caused by the muscle structure in some people's cheeks. But one inventor hoped to make dimples possible for everyone. Evangeline Isabella Gilbert patented her dimple-making machine in 1926. She called her invention the dimpler.

The dimpler consisted of a chin strap and two rubber pieces that were meant to leave indents on each cheek. Gilbert recommended that the dimpler be left on overnight. It was supposed to leave dimple-like indents

SPRAY-ON HAIR

One invention was meant to cover up hair loss for people with thinning hair. In the 1980s, a man named Ron Popeil invented a product he called Great Looking Hair Formula #9. It was also known as hair in a can or spray-on hair. The product became famous because of the infomercials that ran through the 1990s advertising it. The product, which came out of the canister as a liquid, could be sprayed on a person's head. But it was also mixed with powder. This was meant to stick to the existing hair and make it look thicker. The spray-on hair was not permanent and could be washed out. The product was still available for sale in 2025, but it wasn't very popular.

on the cheeks during the day. However, the dimpler was not very comfortable to wear. It also didn't create lasting dimples.

PERMANENT CURLS

Before electric hairstyling tools, people heated irons over a flame to create curls in their hair. For people who wanted long-lasting curly or wavy hair, a woman named Marjorie Joyner invented the permanent wave machine. Joyner patented her invention in 1927. She was the first Black woman to receive a patent.

Damp hair was wrapped around metal rods, which were attached to a dome-shaped machine by electric cords. The hair was then heated to 200 degrees Fahrenheit (93°C). As the hair dried, it would hold the curl. But the hair was left much more brittle afterward. People also risked getting burned. Eventually, new inventions made the curling process safer and easier. As time passed, the permanent wave machine was no longer used in hair salons.

EXPLORE ONLINE

Chapter Three discusses two female inventors. The website below explores more in-depth information about female inventors. As you know, every source is different. How is the information from the website the same as the information in Chapter Three? What new information did you learn from the website?

DIVERSE VOICES: WOMEN INVENTORS

abdocorelibrary.com/weird-inventions

HOUSEHOLD CONVENIENCES

Many inventions have helped make housework easier and less time-consuming. Dishwashers, washing machines, vacuums, and small kitchen appliances all save time and energy for people. Many products are still being invented today that claim to improve people's quality of life at home. Some household inventions intended to make certain tasks more convenient but may have made life more complicated instead.

The invention of various household appliances in the 1900s reduced the amount of hours per week that people spent on housework.

ONION GOGGLES

For some people, the worst part of cooking is chopping onions. When an onion is cut open, it releases chemicals that can cause people's eyes to burn and release tears. In 2006 a company in Columbus, Ohio, invented onion goggles. They are worn like eyeglasses and have a layer of foam around the lenses to keep the chemicals in onions away from the wearer's eyes. The glasses were even featured on popular TV cooking programs hosted by Paula Deen, Rachel Ray, and Martha Stewart.

Some household tasks are never finished. No matter how many times a bed is made, it still needs to be remade every day. The Spanish company Ohea wanted to automate this process. It invented a self-making bed in 2012. It's called a smart bed. The bed features a device that straightens the pillows or blankets back to their original place. The process takes less than a minute.

The bed has two settings. It can be set to automatic so that it makes itself after it senses a person getting out of bed. Users can also activate the device with

Ohea's smart bed wasn't the first self-making bed. In 2008, an Italian inventor showed off his self-making bed at a convention.

a remote. In 2016, the smart bed received quite a bit of attention online. Some people appeared excited about it. Others called it the laziest invention ever. The main drawback to the smart bed is that it doesn't work with regular bedding. The smart bed requires its own specific pillows, sheets, and comforter in order to work.

Although bed glasses are no longer popular, they are still sold today.

BED GLASSES

In 1936, inventor Theodore Hamblin wanted to make reading in bed even more enjoyable. He thought people should be able to read flat on their backs without having to prop up their heads or necks with pillows. So he invented a pair of eyeglasses. These eyeglasses allowed people to lie flat on their backs and still read a book in front of them. The eyeglasses contained mirrors that allowed people to see at a 45-degree angle.

BABY MOP

One company invented a onesie for babies that also acts as a mop. The invention started as a joke. But then people actually started buying and using it. The onesie features soft fabric fringes that are supposed to help dust and mop floors as the baby crawls around. In 2025, the baby mop was sold online for $40. It was available for infants three to twelve months old.

The bed glasses were popular for a short time. They were also known as lazy glasses. For some people, the glasses eased neck pain or strain. But they didn't work well for people who already needed glasses to see.

THE WINDOW BABY CAGE

In the early 1900s, people believed it was important to expose babies to fresh air. They believed this would

Baby cages were inspired by the idea that fresh air purifies the blood of babies.

make babies healthier and prevent them from getting sick. However, in the 1920s and 1930s, more people began moving to cities. This meant people were living close together and in apartments. Fewer people had access to yards or other outdoor spaces.

In 1922, Emma Read patented the baby cage. Her invention was a woven wire cage that could be hung outside windows. Mothers would then place their babies inside the cage to give them fresh air. Baby cages became popular during the 1930s, especially for those living in apartment buildings. As safety concerns arose, baby cages fell out of use.

FURTHER EVIDENCE

Chapter Four has information about inventions that help with household tasks. What is the main point of this chapter? What key evidence supports this point? Go to the article about weird inventions. Find a quote from the website that supports the chapter's main point.

WEIRD BUT TRUE: INVENTIONS

abdocorelibrary.com/weird-inventions

CHAPTER FIVE

FUN AND LEISURE

By the mid-1900s, successful inventions had made life much easier for many people. Modern transportation meant people could travel farther and faster. Household conveniences meant people could spend less time and energy on daily tasks such as cooking and cleaning. This meant people had more time and money to spend on fun. People were looking for new toys, games, and other ways to entertain themselves. Some entertainment inventions turned out to be more strange than fun.

By the 1950s, the television, which had been invented three decades before, became widespread in the United States.

In the 1930s, Hans Laube had an idea for how to change the way people watched movies. Laube thought audience members should not only be able to see and hear the story taking place in front of them but smell it as well. To incorporate smells into movies, Laube created a theater system called the Scentovision. It consisted of a series of pipes running to each seat in a theater. Scents could be released at certain moments during the show through these pipes.

The first Scentovision was shown at the World's Fair in 1939. But the invention's most famous use came decades later in 1960. Film director Michael Todd Jr. wanted to make a movie using the Scentovision, which he had renamed Smell-O-Vision. Laube teamed up with Todd to create the movie, which was titled *Scent of Mystery*. The film premiered in three Smell-O-Vision theaters across the United States in 1960.

People had mixed reactions to the movie. Audience members in the back of the theater received the scents later than those sitting close to the screen.

Hans Laube, *right*, designed a device called the Smell Brain that released the Smell-O-Vision's scents in sync with events in Michael Todd Jr.'s, *left*, movie.

Some viewers said they couldn't smell anything at all. Others complained of a loud hissing sound when the scents were released. Because of technical issues and bad reviews, the movie didn't do very well. It was the only film ever viewed in a Smell-O-Vision.

SMELL-O-VISION
SCENTS

Here are some of the scents released by the Smell-O-Vision during the 1960 screening of the film *Scent of Mystery*. Would you want to smell scents from a movie while you were watching it?

PET ROCKS

Gary Dahl came up with the idea for the pet rock in 1975. The idea was a bit of a joke. The pet rock was advertised as the perfect pet because it didn't need food, water, or training. Dahl sold the rocks in a cardboard carrier box with an owner's manual. They became incredibly popular for about a year. Dahl sold more than one million pet rocks. However, Dahl couldn't patent the pet rock as an invention because rocks are a natural material.

TALKING DOLLS

Thomas Edison was one of the world's most famous inventors. He was born in the United States in 1847. Edison patented more than 1,000 inventions. The improvement of the electric light bulb is one of his most important accomplishments. And his phonograph was the first device capable of recording sound, voices, and music. But many of his inventions are not nearly as well known as the light bulb and phonograph.

Edison was 30 years old when he invented the phonograph. It could record and play back voices and music. Edison decided to harness the new technology in the form of talking dolls. Each doll weighed four pounds (1.8 kg) and stood 22 inches (56 cm) tall. They had wooden limbs and porcelain heads. Inside each doll was a miniature phonograph. A nursery rhyme would play when people turned a crank on the doll's back. The rhymes included "Mary Had a Little Lamb" and "Hickory Dickory Dock." The dolls became available to the public in 1890.

The dolls were not a success. People complained that the music was too quiet and hard to understand. The cranks broke easily, and some dolls didn't work at all. They were also very expensive. Many were returned. They received bad reviews in newspapers. Edison stopped the sale of the dolls only a month after they had been shipped to stores. It's estimated that only about 500 dolls were sold.

Although the talking dolls fell flat, they were still the first commercial product to use recorded sound. And Edison knew that trying and failing was a necessary

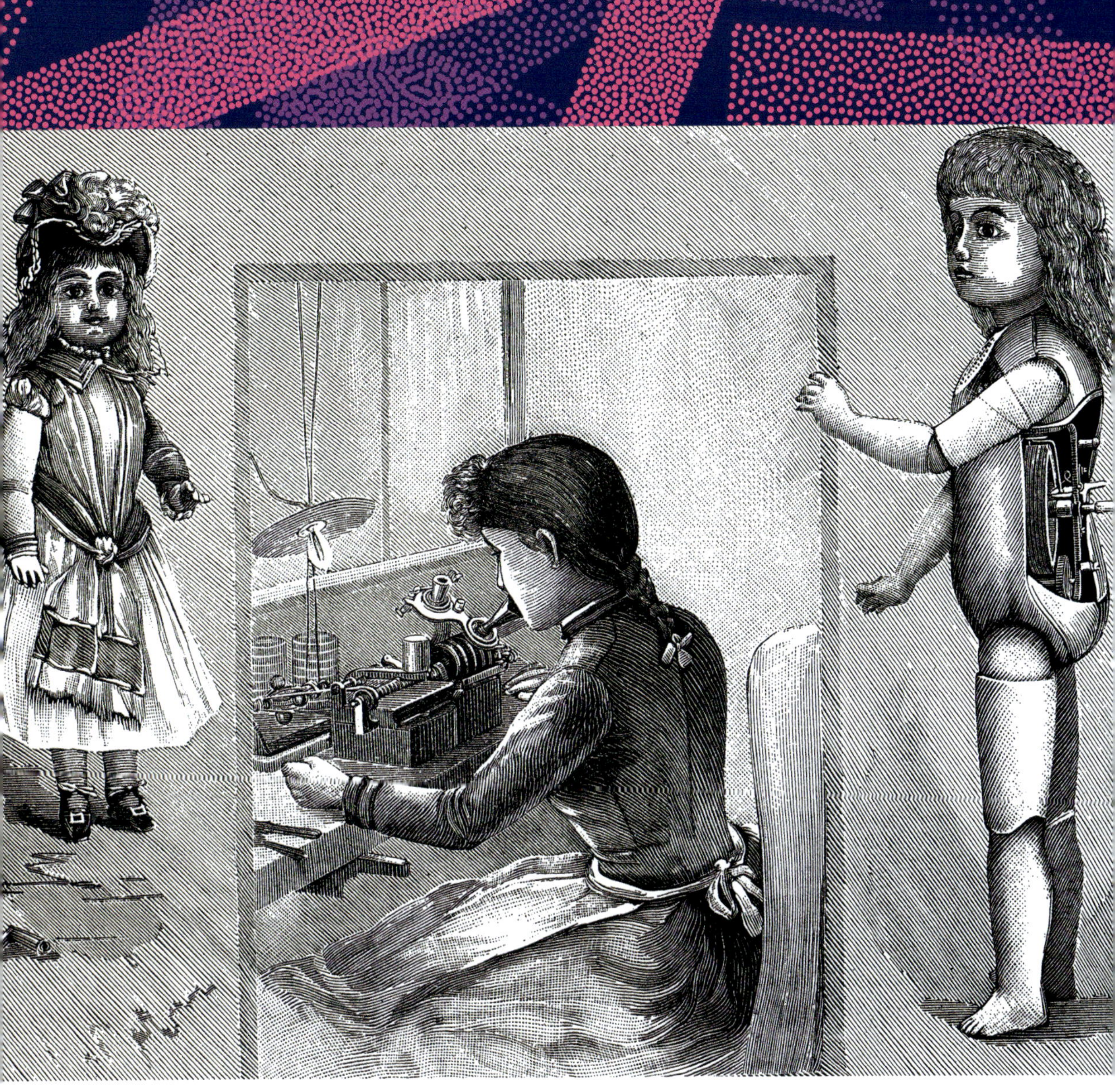

Thomas Edison's talking doll had limbs with joints, allowing children to move its arms and legs.

part of creating new, world-changing ideas. Future inventors would create talking dolls that became very popular.

MR. POTATO HEAD

In 1949, George Lerner wanted to invent a toy that kids could design themselves. He came up with the idea for Mr. Potato Head. The toy came with different plastic body parts attached to pins. The parts included noses, mouths, and eyes. There were also accessories such as hats and glasses. The toy included a Styrofoam potato head, but the instructions let kids know that real potatoes or vegetables would work as well. Later versions included a plastic potato head. The toy remains popular with kids today.

Many inventions have become necessary parts of modern life. People rely on inventions such as the automobile, lightbulb, and internet every day. Not every invention has become as important to people as these. Some inventions strike people as weird and never catch on. But even weird inventions demonstrate the creativity that inventors use to make life easier or more enjoyable.

STRAIGHT TO THE SOURCE

In one interview, Thomas Edison was asked what advice he would give to young inventors. He replied:

I suggest that if the young inventor has an idea he had better reduce it to actual practise and be sure that it works before applying for a patent. Ideas are easy, but working them into commercial shape is generally a long, tedious, and expensive job. . . . Here is where the young inventor will have his greatest disappointment. He will find many a time and, as a matter of fact, in a majority of cases, that the idea has been patented already in one form or another. But disappointments show the salt of the inventor. Only by such disappointments can he triumph finally.

Source: Thomas Edison. "Thomas Edison Speaks to You." *Electrical Experimenter,* Dec. 1919, manifold.umn.edu. Accessed 20 Mar. 2025.

CONSIDER YOUR AUDIENCE

Adapt this passage for a different audience, such as your friends. Write a blog post conveying this same information for the new audience. How does your post differ from the original text and why?

FAST FACTS

- Inventions are machines or creations made by humans to solve problems or make life easier. But not all inventions are successful or stay in use for a long time.
- Leonardo da Vinci sketched out ideas for many different kinds of inventions in his notebook, but most were never actually created. One example is his idea for water shoes.
- Some types of inventions have made travel faster, safer, and more efficient. Other inventions in transportation were more flashy than useful.
- The monowheel and the pramotor didn't turn out to be practical ways to get around. Glowing tires never caught on, either.
- Inventions such as the exercise belt, the dimple-maker, and the permanent wave machine promised to change people's physical appearance but ended up being ineffective or even dangerous.

- Bed glasses, self-making beds, and baby cages set out to solve household inconveniences or problems but may have actually created more work and problems instead.
- Some inventions aim to entertain. But inventions such as the Smell-O-Vision and the first talking dolls were not successful with consumers.
- Some people have invented unique toys such as pet rocks and Mr. Potato Head.

STOP AND THINK

Tell the Tale

Chapter One discusses how Leonardo da Vinci came up with an idea for water shoes. Imagine you are there with him. Write 200 words about what you see.

Dig Deeper

After reading this book, what questions do you still have about inventions? With an adult's help, find a few reliable sources that can help you answer your questions. Write a paragraph about what you learned.

Another View

This book talks about Thomas Edison and his various inventions. As you know, every source is different. Ask a librarian or another adult to help you find another source about this topic. Write a short essay comparing and contrasting the new source's point of view with that of this book's author. What is the point of view of each author? How are they similar and why? How are they different and why?

Say What?

Studying inventions can mean learning a lot of new vocabulary. Find five words in this book you've never heard before. Use a dictionary to find out what they mean. Then write the meanings in your own words and use each word in a new sentence.

GLOSSARY

automate
to alter a process so that it can operate on its own

commercial
designed to make a profit

consumer
a person who purchases products

cosmetic
a product used to improve personal appearance

counterpoise
something that balances something else

infomercial
a television program that promotes a product

pedestrian
a person traveling on foot

principle
a scientific law or idea that explains how something works and why it happens

propel
to push forward

superfluous
going beyond what is necessary

ONLINE RESOURCES

To learn more about weird inventions, visit our free resource websites below.

Visit **abdocorelibrary.com** or scan this QR code for free Common Core resources for teachers and students, including vetted activities, multimedia, and booklinks, for deeper subject comprehension.

Visit **abdobooklinks.com** or scan this QR code for free additional online weblinks for further learning. These links are routinely monitored and updated to provide the most current information available.

LEARN MORE

Buckey, A. W. *Weird Experiments*. Abdo, 2026.

Gagne, Tammy. *Fact and Fiction of American Invention*. Abdo, 2022.

Yenne, Bill. *100 Inventions That Shaped World History*. Sourcebooks, 2023.

INDEX

About the Author

Emma Kaiser is a writer and educator based in western Minnesota. She has a master of fine arts in creative writing from the University of Minnesota, and her writing has appeared in a number of magazines and publications. She is the author of many other nonfiction books for students.